AF375169

To Dream and Be Dreamt

the poetry of

James Stewart

Dedication

This book is Dedicated to the community of friends,
students, loves and lovers who have traveled
this life with James. May this presentation of his words
bring his beauty to us again.

Preface
by Kate Watson

For James Stewart, life was sacred and sensuous, mystifying and miraculous, brimming with meaning and magic. It was a dance, a feast, a holy sacrament. It was friendship and creativity play, the touch of skin on skin and the meeting of hearts. His poetry reflects how he lived, delighting in every extravagance of pattern and rhythm, image and rhyme.

In these verses, whether he is beckoning a lover, gliding and shimmying through a dreamscape, or declaring his presence to all of creation, he doesn't hold back. This is how he demanded to live, how most of the time he did live. It pained him to encounter (in others and himself) the limiting human impulses to defend and to close, to fear and to judge. Marked early in life by societal prejudice (he was Black and gay) and personal tragedy (his sister's death), he was uncompromising in his determination to go deeper, to open wider, to keep challenging and dismantling the barriers of separation.

James relished life and poured himself into it. His enthusiasm was infectious, his sensitivity, acute. Ritual, ceremony, dreamwork, invocation, sacred space—these were as necessary to James as food, both to nourish his spirit and to express his reverence and amazement at all that he saw and experienced. The aspirations and yearnings we hear in his poems would become the gestures he lived by, the gifts he extended, the connections he forged, in seeking to manifest those ideals.

James was an artist, a wounded healer, a dream weaver, threading connections between people and worlds, regardless of differences. Everyone was interesting. "Who is in there?" he would wonder. "Huh? Who is in there?" When you traveled with him in the image world, life was vibrant, startling, tender, funny, buzzing with connections, alive with questions, inviting wonder, inquiry and play.

Empathic and intuitive, he felt the suffering of the world and could offer solace. In my twenties, after taking his Imaginal College, I included these lines in a prose poem: "There are times when I am lost; I fall into confusion or touch some grief in my old soul, and then you drop into silence and listen while I remember and weep, and you do not feel hungry to devour my pain or anxious to patch my wounds; you are simply there like a buoy in the ocean, and sometimes your voice, deep and black and sonorous, resonating from the depths of your heart, tells me you have been where I now am, and you know the strange blend of beauty of pain in the waters where I am voyaging."

When James danced, the whole room danced with him. We had to move—we couldn't help it. When he sang, the room fell silent; we were spellbound. Whether he was singing John Denver's "My Sweet Lady," or "Sweet Little Jesus Boy" at Christmas caroling, or "In My Life" by the great John Lennon, we all stopped and held each other, swaying a little, side to side, our hearts on tiptoe.

When he cooked, he cooked for kings—and served his friends like royalty: chicken melting off the bone; gumbo; collard greens, cornbread and grits; Thanksgiving turkey with all the trimmings; and pies, whole tabletops spread with pies: pumpkin, pecan, apple, rhubarb, berry, lemon—each one made by hand. He had baked into the night...

James was born William James Stewart Jr. on August 16, 1941, in Vicksburg, Mississippi. He graduated from Rosa A. Temple High School in 1959, attended Jackson State University and served in the United States Army (some of the time in Pakistan). He earned a Bachelor of Arts degree from the University of California at Santa Cruz, with an emphasis in Jungian psychology, and throughout his life he remained devoted to offering workshops in dreams and imaginal play. When the Institute of Psycho-Structural Balancing (later renamed the International Professional School of Bodywork), opened in 1977, he joined the faculty, teaching massage therapy combined with consciousness-raising techniques for mind, body, and spirit. James taught at IPSB for decades and was beloved by his students. At his death, the school honored him as "the heart, soul and magic of IPSB." James died at his home in San Diego on August 20, 2016.

Achknowledgements
by John Peterson

I miss the long, rich conversations with James. I miss the many cups of coffee early in the morning and at one point the early morning cocktails. It was a joy to meet up with James on these many get-to-gathers. There was a time when James, myself and Kate Watson formed a poetry performance group. In large part this work came about because of that time. A few years ago, I thought that it would be nice to see James's poetry again. In conversation with Jack Seiliman he got hold of Ed Maupin, found out that Ed had a whole box of James's poetry. I then started the long arduous journey to go through that poetry. And then the pandemic got in the way. Two years without seeing family, or interacting really with anyone, as so many of us know. Slowly going through his work. Finally, I pulled a manuscript together, sent it off to Kate, and Kate took it from there and shaped it into what you see today. So, I have great appreciation to Kate for taking this raw manuscript and shaping it into a manuscript that made sense.

But here's the beauty. I do believe this is a decent look at the beauty of James through his poetry. All of us who knew James recognized that this was a beautiful person, a beautiful man, a beautiful soul, a beautiful body, a beautiful mind, a beautiful spirit. He had the ability to look at life in the most gorgeous way. I miss not having James around, he left us much too soon, and we all are aware of that. And yet he left us with something that doesn't go away. One of the beauties of memory is that when you connect with a memory it becomes the now. It becomes the very moment that you're in. And so, the memory of James, and I hope, seeing his poetry in a book form like this will also bring what we know of James back to us. I think it's something worthwhile. And its been a great honor to be able to do this with Kate and with Jack and Ed. It's been a beautiful process. But I have to admit it has been difficult. In part the difficulty is that I am not as young as I was in those days of glowing beauty with James.

I hope this brings you some joy, some satisfaction
and a renewed appreciation for the Beautiful person that
James Stewart was and is for all of us.

I remember the last meeting that I had with him.
He was already very sick, thankfully I got down to San Diego
to visit with him for a short time. On one of our short walks
through Envision House, he said to me, "I've always had this
beautiful body and for some reason now it is going away
from me." He recognized that he was graced with something
special, a body that was special and yet it was going away
from him. That does seem to be what occurs to all of us. Even
in this beautiful community, Sarah Luth's recent lose points
this out poignantly. And I'm sure we will all pass on our way
towards whatever is, or is not, before us. And we have been
blessed with the community around us, with James amongst
us and yes with life itself. I have been blessed with James and
I give him my love wherever he is, on whatever journey he is
on. I know it will be a beautiful journey. Because he knows
the three things that have taken a prominent place in my life;
they are—Love and Truth and Beauty. And James manifests
all of these in the most glorious way. Thank you, James. I love
you dearly.

Contents

I am a poet.
To find my wings
And to fly into deeper waters
Of Love in fiery splendor
Is my dream.
To melt and flow
In the smoldering honey stream
Of Love.
To singe and burn
And turn
To yearn
To dream and be dreamt
In kaleidoscopic wonder.

Section I

Seeds Sown

The Door

Of all the things on Earth that I desire
To live within the shelter of your love
And move with you as one, like hand in glove
Are what my body, mind and soul require.
For you are everything I most admire
The answer to desire sent from above.
Descending freely like a celestial dove,
You permeate and doth my soul inspire
With depths of pain and heights of joy unknown
Before you came to gently waken me
From dreadful sleep and from the bonds of death
Into new life. Now that the seeds are sown
We'll live each day 'til autumn's jubilee
And dance until we cannot catch our breath.

Immortal Elf

There is a place within that holds itself
aloof from all but you and where I see
a bridging space where you and I must be
to touch the heart of the Immortal Elf.
You stand strong before the mantel shelf
are like the echo of the soul of me
an interface within which I feel free
to fully be the wholeness of myself.
This feeling of an inner light
expands within your quiet embrace
where primal-sounding infinite songs sing.
You are the missing wing the soul takes flight
soaring through a feeling placeless place
I find the tone that makes the Welkin Ring.

Across the Room

Across the room is much too far
and distant for an avatar
to lounge in lengthy, seductive pose
the rooster's signature exposed.
Look out! Your zipper's showing, perhaps
I should be going.

Across the room is much too far
a distance for a jaguar
sleek and radiant, alluring cat
Strike that pose! I like it like that.
To bolt or flee, no longer my desire
I willingly succumb to the Sacred Fire.

Across the room is much too far
I desire you closer than you are.
To touch, to hold you near to me
To feel, to know, and also see.
But there is no substitute for this
the eternal caress, the breathless kiss.

I cross the room to where you are
No longer wishing upon a star.
Holding, I'm held in your embrace
Spirit waters pervade this space
I feel unraveled, I am undone
Yet within this place we fuse as one.

You cross the room to where I am
And like a primal Abraham
Establish a cornerstone in me
A foundation woven of I and thee.
And from the bliss of our perfection
A Universal resurrection.

Mirroring Waters

On the shore of the mirroring waters
I lay me down
And rest within
The quiet reflection
Of your tenderness.

In child-like awe
I touch the crystal surface
And watch us shimmer
Into a thousand beautiful dreams
And remembrances
Of familiar times
Enchanted by the Love between us.

Your cooling moistness
Melts my fiery heart
And I sleep
Within the gentle caress
Of your liquid diamond body's
Moving stillness
As the misty morning breeze
Breathes the golden sun
Into the yawning windows
Of·our souls' first awakening
And kisses our dawning eyes
Into the recognition
Of our unitary bliss.

I give thanks to the Sacred Springs
That nourished this bountiful pool
And to the mystery
That led me to its shores.

Imaginings April 10

Through melting diamond tears
My eyes perceive a vision
Of crystal purity.

I carry you within me
As a weight and an inspiration.
Your presence a pungent fragrance
Permeates the warp and woof
That is the tapestry of my soul.

I melt intoxicated
Into enchanting dreams
That call me into soft receiving shoulders
And lips that slide, suck and murmur
In liquid labial evocation
Of deep cellular dreams
And nuclear memories.

The future possibilities
Of generations spun
In the dewy web
Of our splendid love.

Imaginings April 11

Happy my heart
The moment the day
Embraced and held me
In its gentle light.
Veiled in misty shroud
My heart paints with colors
That Love's memories forgot
And caresses the Light
With creamy Darkness.
We roll across a meadow green
And quench our thirst with midnight dew
As Love changes water into wine.

Of Balance

I sing to you of balance
But do you hear my song
Or merely the echoes
Of past memories:
Conclusions drawn and set
In final form for all time.

You speak of balance
As some kind of stasis
A static, dead something.
How blind you seem to wogie:
The physical body in its
Awesome balance
An infinity of Yin-Yang
In one:
Systole-diastole
Inbreathing-outbreathing
Alkaline-acid
All dynamic movements of balance
All contained within One.

Even Kabir perceived:
I am a woman and the wife of God.

The Emptiness

On a fresh, clear spring morning
A moist, fallow, fertile field
Lying naked in the sun
Whose brilliant rays of light and heat
Evoke the seeding life
Hidden within my furrows.

The emptiness created by your absence
Is a nest in which I discover
The subtle facets
Of my love for you.

Missing you
Is half the pleasure
Of loving you.

Your absence is a blessing
That reveals
The farther reaches
Of our love.

Your absence is a mirror
In which I see reflected
Hidden depths and meanings
Of Love.

Missing you
Is half the discovery
And realization
Of my love for you.

Your love is like a bridge
That leads into the ever-renewing mists
Of creativity.

With steady pace
The pre-dawn mists march
Through canyon depths
And fill my soul
With fertile fetal fetishes
Of luminous morning light.

My Friend

My friend,
My brother,
My Love,
Don't let the shape
Of boxes
Or the illusion
Of necessity
Bury the song
Of the mountain wind
That breathed our hearts
Into such close proximity.

Upon mountain pinnacle's altar
Between blossoming wild flowers
And fragrant scrub
A bed is laid.
The wind prepares
Its subtle celebration:
Two hearts
Falling
Slowly,
haltingly
But inevitably falling
Toward the pinnacle.
Softly,
Gently
Falling
Toward the point
Of reluctant
Inevitable merging

Where the Holy Wind
Is nourished
By the breath
We breathe into
And upon
Each other
As we touch
And hold
Each other
In half-moon's
Luminous light.

The mountain creatures dance.
On the foot of our bed
They dance.
In celebration
They dance
The long awaited dance
Of blending.
The blending that
Creates a door
Through Nature
Which oozes
Into new realities.

Moonlight welcomes
The dawning sun
As through the mists
Two lizards lie
In perfect harmony.

Imaginings May 8

My Love, You say you love me
Yet little by little I feel your love
Shrink into convoluted rooms and tunnels
That stifle and choke
The crystal river of life-giving waters
That surge through the canyons
Of my breathless soul.

You say you love me
And yet I see that love
As but a subtle lasso
To capture my soul
And corral it
In your fearful vision
Wherein I would be fed
In measured increments
Of makeshift tenderness
While the pulsing life
Within my cells turns sour
From lack of bold expansive Love.

You say you love me
And yet your love
Is a fearful shield
To hide the urge of Life
And a sword
To kill the spark
With promises of
Domesticated bliss.

Mine, my Love, is the way
Of the soaring falcon
Who in subtle softness
Rides the currents of breath
That carries it to the farthest
Reaches of space
And swoops mightily to earth
To perch gently
On tender branches
and sings its song of freedom
That is carried on the wind
And catalyzes all life
With its radiant sound.

Listen with your heart, my Love
That fear may not enshroud
You with its hypnogogic murmurs
That would magically transform
Me into a malevolent demon
with forbidden raptures
That awakens you from sleep.
Listen with your heart, my Love
With your heart
With your heart.

September 14

My Friend, I want you to know
That despite the fear, pain and passion
Despite the flashes of searing anger,
Despite the emotions and drama,
There is love
Love for the boy
Love for the boy-man
And Love for the man.

Perhaps the dream of deeper meeting
Must wait for another time and place.
Perhaps that meeting has already happened
In the deep, more invisible places
Within our souls, who knows?
It's always the dream of what could have been
That hurts the most.
I remember YOU.

September 16

Speak to me, relentless pain,
Let me hear your story,
Sing to me your song
That I may know
The voice of the Invisible.

October 3

There is really nothing I can say
Words just seem to get in the way
Therefore, in silence I carry the space
Between us to Earth, to Nature
And ask her to do what She will
To bear witness to this process.

November 11

Fire and water reluctantly meet
In a shadow dance on the plain.
The world stops at dusk
Sun pauses in multi-hued silence
And casts a spell of magic
That alters time and space
And through the interface
We slip into a realm
Between sun and moon
And light and dark,
A camper's heater provides the spark
As we make our bed
Upon the firm and stony ground
Inside the earth-toned veils
That are the delicate caldron
Wherein we pour our fragmented
And dismembered souls
As a holy offering
To moonlight winds.

Inside, where we are thrown
Upon each other and down
To plain, repugnant ordinariness,
How can I escape your relentless
Call to depth?
How can I escape from myself?
Separation is but a trick I play
To give myself a sense of independence,
the sense of pain and sterility
Only serve to drive me
Home again.

Home...
Where the sea between us
Ebbs and flows in seasonal rhythms
Of you and me
Of man and woman
Of friend and foe
Of man and man
Of children playing
In fantastic worlds
Of endless dreams
Spun from the threads
Of our eternal, simple
And ordinary embrace.

Stillness

A stillness
A soft, quiet stillness
Blending smoothly
Effortlessly into living memories
Of how we have been in love.

I see you
A veil has lifted
You melt into flowing fragrances
Intimate dreams
Of past and future times
Wherein we deftly move
Through interface
Of infinite worlds.

Together we play
Eternal variations
On a single theme
Of how we can be
You and me
Constantly giving birth
Elsewhere and here on Earth
To the children
Of our Love and Unity.

How Long My Soul has Waited

How long my soul has waited
To feel again the deep caress
Of penetrating tenderness
Companions in the infinite round
Turning, yearning, burning
Learning anew how our hearts
Find where we belong.
Eternal pulsing magic dance
Of you and me
Of we.
Of Us, a cornerstone
From which the world arises
Multifaceted disguises
Heightening intrigue
Just to prove to ourselves again
How inevitably
We are one.
Of Bountiful Harvest.

December 2

Do I want it to be you?
Do I want it to be you?
Do I want it to be you?
Which you?
Which one of you?
All of you?
Yes, all of you.
Especially the you
That stands behind
The cobwebbed gate
Amidst greying shadows
That shroud colorful vistas
Of fecund fantasies
Moving landscapes and shifting dimensions
Woven in the rhythms of heartbeat and breath
And dancing to the sensual pulse
Of you and me
Of we
Of us inside
The crystal egg
Of spaceless space
That radiates and reverberates
Worlds of creation's mysteries.

December 2 Again

You are a quiet fire
That burns within my soul
A flickering golden yellow flame
Sensually swaying
A camel in a desert caravan
Smoothly riding the heated wind.
Late afternoon sun melts
And drips its honey tears
Upon the rising dunes
Beside the precious waters
In this timeless oasis
Beneath the orange-gold dusky sky
We make our bed.

Water touches fire
The mists arise
Delicately woven veils
Softly conceal the splendor
Of our radiant nakedness
Night winds mold the undulating desert
Into trickling streams
That flow upon impassioned breath
Raindrops oozing from my skin
You drink my silent tears.

The Serpent Arises

As the ancient serpent arises
And the dance of the veils begins
Through icy floes
Memory grows
Desert wisdom peeks through
Astronauts explore
Another space that is you.

Looking far
Looking near
In the center
Still waters appear
Three quarters of the quadrants done
The fourth a birthing of the one
Growing fetus embraces the image stream
As we patiently await the birthing of the dream.

The lion appears a messenger of the sun
A mummy appears the unraveling has begun
A thawing as sacred waters not flow
Fire and ice the serpent is on the go.

Things are moving, the circle not quite complete
In the center the shadow child quietly takes a seat
Awaiting the birthing of itself--
The return of the elusive, immortal Elf
And in the center the magnificent Earth
Coming into cosmic birth.

Cocoon

The circle turns and once again
I find an empty boredom
It's over and there is nothing more to say.
We, we sit in utter fear, hoping beyond hope
That things are not what they seem
And yet it is clear
There is nothing here
But empty fantasies gazing across a chasm
And lingering in atrophied dreams that never quite were
And never will be
For these worlds can never cross.
Thus the loss
The pain and bewilderment
Or just bewilderment of an unanswerable "Why?"
And sitting and sighing like an oracle of old
Objective and unmoved
I peer into the veil of future selves
And wonder what costumes there are now to be worn.
Shorn of my illusions I nakedly stand
And know that all the while
The feelings have never been wrong.
The fantasy of unity dissoloves in the mists
And I wait for the possible doorway
Into another unknown adventure.

Section II

Beloved

Abdullah

While playing on the branches of the Tree of Life,
Through leaf and limb I view the Earth below.
You and I, Conchita,
We dance down the curling of the Holy Vine
To stand upon the Sacred Ground
Enshrouded in the moon's luminous light,

Upon the blue-grey moonscape
a piece of Arab earth
to see in surreal splendor.
As I sit upon the three-pronged pruned
Branches of the Holy Vine,
You, Abdullah, approach
From a distant, vast spaciousness
Emerging from the Arabesque fragment
Of the Arabian life stream.

My brother, my friend, my teacher
I welcome you into my soul
As you welcome me into your house.
How surprised I am to find you here
At the root of the Holy Vine.

Conchita, you did not tell me
That such a friend would be here...

And with eyes that play knowingly
You respond with a magical glance
That is a secret mystery
Of the serpentine motions
Of the Sacred Fire.

My brother, myself.
O gentle strength,
You are the rock and the water
And the action of the water upon the rock.
You are love and compassion.
You are the strong bull
that bears the Holy Flame.
You are the seer and the poet;
But more than this you are poetry
Emanating into "unfathomable" forms,
To those who have forgotten the timeless
Hieroglyphic images that are the
Eternal language of the soul.

Your body is the Living Fountain.
Your body is the Living Spring
Flowing into time and space
And revealing the ancient message
That in its newness
Burns a path of timeless truth
Through fruitless harvests of idolatry.

Lead me into your house, my brother,
That I may learn from you
And grow in your fertile presence.

An Opening

Through an opening
in the city wall I peer.
Silently watching the movements
As the city-dwellers are about
Their daily chores, the acts of living.

Crystal Vines

Crystal vines entwine
Your soul, my soul, our soul, one soul
silver, moonlit night.

The meadow melted
Into silent streams flowing
Through our loving hearts.

We walk in twilight
The wind, our silent partner
Breathes us into one.

Pines sing the wind's song
You cradled in my body
Half-moon's light reveals.

Two divine beings
Weave a song of moonlight winds
Luminosity.

Candlelight's shadow
Anoints us with golden threads
Tenderness and bliss.

Morning mist arises
Tenderness in dawning eyes
Two melt into one.

Between our body
Flaming fingers touch and melt
Molten icy tears.

The Fire

The fire burns:
The fragrance of human flesh
Inflamed with Love.

Body the incense
Heart afire with flaming Love
Cooling, tender Love.

Wind incites the embers
Irresistible passion
Roaring flames that burn.

Love's a desert fire
Parching, burning, calling
The waters of Death.

Probing Fire Bird
Feeling my inner contours
Beneath moving wings.

Talons grip and tear
Tender wings caress my soul
Cradled on hawk's winds.

November 26

Beloved,
The Autumn morning sun
Upon my skin
Warmly wakens memories
Of our bodies melting,
Merging and mingling
In quiet tenderness.

Come again, my Love
Come again and find me
The path is clear
And I'm so easy.

Let me see that smile
Let me feel that glow
The glow of you touching me
Touching you, touching me...

Laugh, my Love.
Run naked in your laughter.
Let them glimpse the glow
And know
That you and I are One.

November 29

Beloved,
Lying near your heart
You touching me touching You...
Just remembering.

Morning near your heart
You touching me touching you...
Simply being us.

Morning near your heart
You touching me touching you...
O magic mirror.

Dawning with our hearts
You touching me touching you...
Mirror moon magic.

Life's magic mirror
You touching me touching you...
Dawn's reminiscence.

Lying so near you
Moon miracle magic man
Mirroring we dance.

Rust red dawning sky,
Touch me deep where soul fires burn
And yearn's for your Love.

Dawning Power

The waking canyon
Observes me standing amidst
Its dawning power.

My hawk consciousness
Flies above silent canyons
seeing with my eyes.

Eyes of dawn's first blush
Looking at my tender soul
Moving with the Wind.

Misty drops of tears
Arising from morning's eyes
Purify my soul.

Another dawning
Fills my life with melting light
Love's waters flowing.

Pre-dawn silences.
In the canyons of my soul
Morning spirits sleep.

Misty golden dreams
Memories of ancient times
Reverberating.

Steel and concrete masks
Intimidating costumes
To cloak the Oneness.

Behind shirt and tie
He stands hidden, embedded
In concrete costume.

Darkest, longest night
Miracle, luminous light!
Yes, the child is born.

To Move with You

Beloved,

To move with you, to dance with you; to live a living poetry with you is what my heart desires. To know you intimately and deeply and multifacetedly is my dream. Reveal to me the path of Love, reveal to me the path of Unity. Teach me to love in Unity. Let me understand that I am now living and experiencing Humanity's dream of Unity. Reveal to me the oneness of my breath, of night and day, of sun and moon, of masculine and feminine, of right and left, of up and down, of life and death.

I feel you in my heart, my blood, my body. I feel you riding in me, rising in me. You are like this woman, this voluptuous woman who loves much and many. And I must admit that you make me nervous. How can you love so many and so intimately? I am human, be merciful. Help me to be true to myself.

January 5

Inside,
Inside Beloved.
You are no longer a dream.
For I hold you inside
As a mother holds a newborn child.
I hold you in my heart:
An awesome living reality.

Inside, Beloved,
You are alive
And growing
Inside
Me.

A Sea

My heart is like a moving sea
Whose ebb and flow
Is spun from magic tears
Of melting diamond dreams.

Who are you, vulnerable lady
Wearing your heart like a trophy
A badge of your earning power.
Who are you, tender lady?
Illustrated lady, who are you?
A woman longing for a man;
A woman who wants to feel the fire
Make the fire come alive
Fan the flames
Feel the heat
Take my softness
It's your hardness
Magical permutations.
I bear you
You give birth to me.
O hidden wound

Beloved

Beloved,
Will you let me go so easily
Will you let me shut the door?
Will you let me stop the flow of Love's sweet joy?
Will you let me pass as just a memory?
A dream tucked away
In a basement
In a box marked "unimportant"?

Will you let me stop our gentle song?
Will you let me cut off our wonder
And the magic only we can create?
Will you?
Will you?

Will you let me block a thousand years of loving?
Will you let my jealousy ruin us?
Will you let my confusion cast a shadow
On our brilliant light?
Will you let our discovery of each other end?
Will you?
Will you?

Will you let the fires die?
Will you believe my obvious lie?
Will you forget the way I cry?
Will you?
Will you?

Will you take me at my word?
I can't believe that, it's too absurd.
Or will you be a strong fire bird
And win me?

A Fine Musical Instrument

Beloved,
like a fine musical instrument
You hold me in your masterful hands
And with the Beauty of your genius
Evoke sounds and tones
Impossible to imagine.

I quiver and resonate
As memories of intimate worlds unfold
Between the realities
Of wakeful sleep
And surrealistic dreams.

I merge and blend
In harmonic overtones
Of multidimensional awe
As my cells unfurl the shimmering tapestry
Our golden sun dance
Of silver moonlit nights.

Soft breezes whisper
Starlight landscapes' secret songs
And murmurings of quiet delight
As we pulse and throb
In cyclic harmony.

Beloved, Let us sing a song
Unheard by human ears
Unfelt by human hearts.
With radiant song
Let us create a sound
That moves the deepest cells

To rhythmic swaying
To and fro.
A magic dance
Enchanting creature codes.
Between the visible space
Let magic irradiate light
Suffuse the spaceless space
With creativity's irresistible presence.

Beloved, the presence of your radiant light
Unlocks the doors of my feminine soul.
I stand revealed
Naked
Enchanted by your irradiance.

A Fabric Woven

How I long to tell
        Of the subtle stirrings
In my soul.
        Yet when I speak
The voice of Truth Eludes me.

How I long to speak
        To sing of the joy
That you have brought me
        In the tenderness
Of your Love.

How I long to sing
        Of how well we fit,
Of sparkling lights
        Of the magic mirror dance
Of you and me.

Of how we See,
        Sense, touch, taste
And interlace.
        We:
A fabric woven in ancient times
        Whose warp and woof
Is ever new

        As we weave Us again:
A Variation on the theme
        Of timeless Love.

Let Me Bear

Don't let me forget, Beloved,
Keep me from the dreaded state of slumber
Wherein I die the death of lethargy.
Open my eyes, my mind,
And especially my heart
That I may live in constant awareness
Of the Mystery of Being.
Let me see with the eyes of my heart;
That I may pierce the veils of Maya

And behold the eternal movement-stillness of the
Invisible. Let me stand on the edge of Oblivion
And wrest out of Nothing
Morsels of Living Truth
Whose bitter-sweetness shall be food
To satisfy the hunger and quench the thirst
Of my comrades.

Or if it pleases Thee
Let me be like the moon which of itself is nothing
But in its fullness blesses
With its light
Illuminating the night

Let me bear
Whatever is to be,
And let me fill
And fulfill
My part in that Being.

Section III

Rising Up

Frankincense Road

On the road of frankincense
I contemplate my experience.
A priest blesses the lad's dance
While things mushroom as I glance.

Events seem to be coming to a head
I hope my accounts aren't in the red!
Bear meets fawn on the road,
Penguin looks on from their abode.

Direction is needed to get it right
Will this be an encounter, a sheer delight?
The workers seem to get what they try
To clean up after whatever they ply.

And does that man belong to this scene?
It is happening behind him, if you get what I mean.
The plane seems to be riding the temple of fire
That's all I can say, so I'll just retire.

Rising Up

Rising up from deep below
Velvet darkness strikes a blow
Disruptive in its timely flow
Inspiring awareness and the desire to know.

In the rising, armor falls
Much too heavy to hold the call
And in its wake, metal and water arise
Omens for the coming surprise.

Black and White

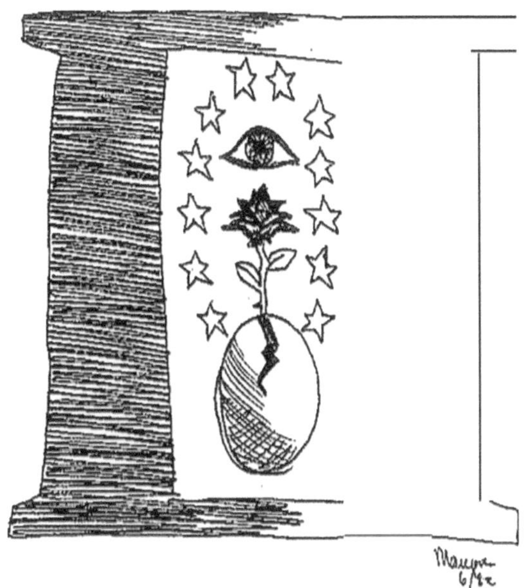

Within the containment of black and white
within the interplay of dark and light
The birthing has begun.

A gateway reveals a starry shield
Consciousness arises, dark and light yield
A blossoming of the One.

Signature of Eleven, Eleven
doorways open to galactic heaven
separation is undone.

Between the pillars of black and white
within the womb of dark and light
dimensional infusion has begun.

A Song of Equinox

Once again Life falls in equal measure
Yang and Yin a balanced, priceless treasure.
Too soon transformed into another play
Directions change, new path the inner way.
The turning leaves a variegated hue
reflected in the dance of I and you.
Cycles spent on a helical merry-go-round
the seasons' shimmerings displayed upon the ground.
Again a still point's reached within the dance
and new directions are spawned by wily Chance.
Our greening shifts to yellow, bronze and gold
new stories rise insisting to be told.
Anxious permutations spiral dancing
shape-shifting metamorphic dreams enhancing
a glowing harvest moon the landscape lights
night birds prepare for dark and moonlit flights
into the mystery of velvet black
whose bosom holds the gifts the light worlds lack
Tomorrow we unfold into the deep
and enter the forbidden, ancient Keep
where things are never ever what they seem
the golden key in that place is the dream.
So onward into autumn again we fly
and drinking deep we disappear——we die
as quiet whispers sweetly spin their spell
tones come alive from deep within the well.

The silent seed, the shuddering, sagacious sound
and birth again emerges in the Round
a light is spent, the luminous waters flow
the darkness stirred reveals an inner glow
and mysteriously visions begin to grow
into other places within this time
and into other times within this place
a dimensional shift, we find the interface
and marvel at the liquid light of grace.
So once again Life falls in equal measure
Yin/Yang is one—a rich and priceless treasure.

September 19

Breakthrough!
The living flame does oversee
Into the left and out of the right
The merging together, the coming to be
Into the left and out of the right.

Greening dragon breathes the flame
Into the left and out of the right,
As queen of the deep remembers the name
Into the left and out of the right.

Wooden serpent to the blossom bows
Into the left and out of the right
The resurrected temple of the heart allows
Into the left and out of the right

Into the left and out of the right
The slithering serpent clears the sight
Bronze gold feather poised for flight
Into the left and out of the right
Into the left and out of the right
Into the left and out of the right.

Fairy speaks with rising heart
Ancient temple commands a part
Reveal your presence within this play
Sealing the dawning of a newborn day.
Ring the bell and sound the horn
Celebrate what is shorn
Embracing what is born.
Into the left and out of the right
Into the left and out of the right.

Imaginings April 10 6:30 am

I am woman.
I am soft, subtle, silent
And strong.
I am like a mirror
I reflect all in reverse.
I am like dark serene waters
Half revealed at the mouth
Of a cave.
Inside
I harbor the mystery of darkness.
And the hidden splendor
of the midnight sun.
Within the shroud of darkness
I am the keeper of dreams.

I am an ephemeral treasure
A shape-shifting chameleon
Whose diffusive elusiveness
Is rooted in dark depths.

I am the night sky
That brings forth and holds the stars.
I am the bright blue canopy of heaven
That embraces the sun.
I am the bountiful earth
That bodies forth and sustains all things.

I am the dream weaver.
I am the benevolent sorceress
Who brings forth your every wish.
My body encompasses you.
I am the very ground you walk upon.

I am the food you eat.
I am the stage upon which
You play out your existence.
I am the room in which you live.
I am the tomb in which you lie.

I am the stuff of which your life is filled.
It is my blood that nourishes you
Even in your wildest dreams.
I am the hammer and the nail
And the idea behind the hammer and the nail.
But most of all
I am Love.

It is not my wish to frighten you.
I am soft, subtle, silent and strong.
I can be led
But I will not be driven.

Intentional Renewal

I intend to enter a heightened state.
I intent to touch the hand of fate.
I intend to contact creatures divine
With the galactic web I intend to align.

I intend to anchor within the Dreamtime.
My life is a song of melody and rhyme.
I intend to surf the Zuvuya
and leave appropriate portals ajar.

I intend an eternal hookup clear.
I intend to live in many worlds without fear.
I intend to harmonize inside and out.
I intend to live without any doubt.

I intend to radiate the evolutionary Light
Each day to feel it luminous and bright.
I intend to live life as a unified dream
nurtured by experience of the Cosmic Beam.

I intend a shaman of the dreaming to be
To resonate the tonal quality called free.
I intend to enliven my world with Love
I intend to harmonize below/above.

I intend to live synchronously
Fully honoring the consciousness I am created to be.
I intend to merge with the Archetypal Healer.
I intend to be an articulate feeler.

I intend to ride the sound of Om
Within each fractal resonance "at home."
In whatever dimension I find myself to be
I anchor there in resolute safety.

I intend to center my consciousness
Embrace multidimensionality in deep caress.
Aesthetically blending below and above
I intend to harmonize myselves in Love.

I intend to manifest the fullness of my potential
to exuberantly live the Quintessential.
Exploring and discovering in joy and fun,
I intend realization of the Presence of One.

Mother's Day, May 12

This elaboration of two descriptive words
(Mother's Day) is, in a nutshell, an explorative, heuristic
way of beginning to see the stories that dreams are more
deeply and with greater richness, made of. We can take the
words at face value and within the context of their current
usage, yet words, like people, have an origin and history;
their birth is an evolution. And to merely skim the surface
is to not see the complex and elegant tapestry that imbues
words with color and richness of meaning. As the tapestry
becomes clear, roads open for us in myriad directions.
The same association and analogy can be made about the
dreamer and the dream - the dream is to the dreamer as
the word is to its origin and history. Without the origin
and history of the dreamer to fill out the dream code, the
dream remains just that, an undeciphered code. The very
being and experience of the dreamer is the key of access.

Dreams are stories that emerge from our own
darkness and even the responses they evoke in us can
be an access point into relationship with this seeming
autonomous creative power inside each of us. When we
start simply with a typical verbal evocation and explore
and circle it, two simple words have opened us into a
creative process that's engaging, expansive and hopefully
fun and enriching. Through paying attention, perhaps we
can come to an experience of how "the little leaven leavens
the whole loaf," or "how the still, small voice" speaks with
unimaginable richness. Dream images can be just that:
compact, concentrated, brimming with energy and the

encoding power of our own histories. If we merely skim
the surface by not taking the time (whatever the reason or
excuse), then the richness right under our noses, in our
own backyards, so to speak, is missed, repressed through
lack of attention, not seen (Nazi-en). And how subtly and
skillfully we Nazi (not see, i.e., ignore, suppress) ourselves.
There is a saying, "He that is ignorant of his-story is
doomed to relive it."

God's Gift

Me and the Wind

Me and the wind are one
Me and the wind are one
Me and the wi-i-ind,
We are one.

Me and the wind are one
Me and the wind are one
Me and the wi-i-ind,
We are one.

Me and the tree are one
Me and the tree are one
Me and the tree-e-e,
We are one.

Me and the tree are one
Me and the tree are one
Me and the tree-e-e,
We are one.

Me and the brother are one
Me and the brother are one
Me and the brother-er,
We are one.

Me and the sister are one
Me and the sister are one
Me and the sister-er,
We are one.

WE ARE ONE, WE ARE ONE
We ARE ONE!

WE ARE ONE, WE ARE ONE
WE ARE ONE!

Bridge: When you think with your head
         and not your heart
         You will surely miss the best pa-a-art.

Me and the wind are one
Me and the wind are one
Me and the wi-i-ind,
We are one.

WE ARE ONE, WE ARE ONE
WE ARE ONE!

WE ARE ONE, WE ARE ONE
WE ARE ONE!

Unencumbered Vessel

I am an unencumbered vessel of Love and Beauty,
Creativity and Abundance, and I inseminate my
environment, wherever I may be, with those qualities
without draining myself. I know Life is Abundant and
Everlasting.

I have a quick, agile mind. I am insightful and ingenious. I
am filled with constructive, creative ideas. I am a poet and
a singer. I reflect the divine through my creative expression.
And most of all I love profoundly and abundantly.

I am a lover. I am as clear as quartz crystal.

I am sovereign in my essential being. I lean on no one, save
myself. I am love: love of myself in all of my aspects and
possibilities. I am beautiful. I embrace the beauty of myself
without comparison with others. I am all that I am and
that is wonderful.

The spirit of myself, the Logos Spermatikos, irradiates my
world, and the seeds of my becoming emerge in the fertile
soil of my desires and spring forth in the wilderness of
future selves—dazzling, alive, abundant, ecstatic and
joyfully free. As a dream-art scientist I traverse the hidden
places in myself and create worlds of sensual, magical
delight that nourish the heart and enlighten and enhance
the experience of the world.

I am a lover. My heart-soul weaves songs and melodies
whose subtle sounds caress the souls of my brothers and
sisters in a mutual recognition unspeakable, yet sacred
and true in their emotive power, evoking memories of
celebrating around the Sacred Fire.

I am enormously successful without credentials. I possess
all the resources I need to do what I want.

I am free, alive, healthy and nourishing All That I Am.

Only One Night

There is only one night
and we circle it to uncover
or rediscover dreams
woven from a heart's desire
that stoke the fires of a
passion born of future memories
luminous with the radiance of pure love
remembered as life-giving sound
emitted by a mystery impossible to understand

Suspended

When I am in a place like this
Suspended, reserved, alone
A skillfully constructed instrument
Seemingly without a tone.
I wonder, knowing that it is all just fine
Yet knowing this, wander down a line
Into a vast, suspended place
Without a face
Or subtle trace
Of who I was or am
But still I know
That I am
Within and outside of this moment of sensation
And now to seed a recreation
That leads again to unknown places
Fashioning new and different faces
Truly reflecting an undiscovered me
Realized and free.

Section IV

Song of Me

Birth

Baptised in the waters of forgetfulness
I play a game of pretending that I've lost
myself in order to find myself again.
The problem with pretending is
what you think you are, you are,

The tidal waters of forgetfulness, the hypnotic veil of sleep
I awaken into a world whose currents ebb and flow
in unknown rhythms they wax and wane
and being out of harmony confusion reigns.

In a tumbling tidal wave
I am cast upon an unknown shore
broken and split I find myself cradled in the arms
of a strange, soft creature, helplessly in need.

I touch and feel.
A plethora of sensations drowns the vision
of who I am—I drink and drown.
Another current rises and swells and in its veils
opaque memories of distant times brush across
the canvas of my mind.
The artist's brush an umbilical
across a threshold into forever.

Fleeting images dance upon the stage of my feeling
reminding me of presentiments that fade with time
as I fall into delicious sleep tugging at a warm,
soft, nourishing breast.
I willingly tuck the timeless behind me
and in blindness I awaken.

Twenty-Seven

Twenty-seven
        Two and seven,
Nine and completion
        Of round one.
Twenty-seven
        Ides of March
Burst of Spring
        Nineteen seventy
Birth,
        Birth in the depths
A Great Phallus
        Plunging in violent
Tenderness
        Velvet hands
Searching blindly
        For the Holy Place.
Throbbing, persisting
        Opening
Forgotten cavernous
        Chambers, rooms
Of distant dreams
        Memories of ancient
Cellars and dungeons
        Darkened in the
Forgetfulness of Ages.

Liquid fire
        Pouring down the
Dark ravines
        Of my soul
Sure to find its
        Resting place
Behind the skin
        Of phantasmagoria

Lighting up the
                The hidden crevices
Awakening the Greater Man
                living within
The Primeval forest.

Liquid fire
                Melting my will
And my strength
                With voluptuous rhythms
Of Love and Magic.
                Burning and cooling
Undulating purple serpent
                DNA and RNA.
Androgynous serpent
                Unfolding your undulating
Female
                And your male of stone
And yet you are yourself

Offering

On this Red Crystal Earth Day
On this Portal Day
I desire to gather my harvest for this yearly season
And sort through and assimilate
What wisdom I have gained

I desire to interface with the dimension of healing
And to confer with the healing elders
Past and future
For myself and all my relations.

I desire to contribute to the current enlightenment
Unfolding upon the planet
Through my own self-healing and clearing
And through making myself available
To be a channel of blessing
To myself and all my relations.

I desire to become "accustomed" to the state of Light
And to stabilize my conscious presence there.

I desire to contribute to and help facilitate
The dawning of the Age of Aquarius.

I desire to be honest with myselves
And to create a gathering of community
Where all express and contribute with equal voice.

I desire to be open to and receive what is necessary
For this point in my journey
And I desire to know the degree to which I am a healer
On the lines of time.

I desire to grow in my understanding and experience of
Love Unconditional.

I desire to be wholly present and courageous
In exploring parallel worlds and non-locality.

Blessed be the body, I am
Blessed be the mind, I am
Blessed be the soul, I am
Blessed be the spirit, I am
Blessed be the Oneness and Unity, I am
Blessed be the tao, I am.

Song of Me

Through endless days I sing the song of Me.
Through dream~filled nights still, the song of Me,
Delightful me
Frightful me Insightful me.
I speak the sound of Me
                              Free
To be
I see
                              Me.

O Me me "me"
How can it be?
I searched so diligently for
                              Thee
To discover Only "me"
                              Free
In the knowledge of me
Awakening I find not you
But Me
A song that is a dream
Embracing so called You
For there's no you
But "me"

The Cult of You
A sleight of mind
A mere turn in the mirror
Oh
                              Me

How preceptively
The trick is played
A trick of fear
Lest I discover
                              Me

Too much to know
That I alone am free
That what is so-called
                     Thee
Is merely
                     Me.

I searched for You
In endless apparitions
Time and again
I find in you
The Great Betrayer
For you can only be
A part of Me
The serpent bites his tail
To taste the truth:
That in the devouring of myself
I am awakened to the wonder
And the Mystery
Of
                     Me

Infinite Me

Me!
How fresh and ever new.
Singing I dance the infinite embrace
Of Me.
My perimeter is nowhere
For I am everywhere.

O the shock!
O the terror!
O the shocking, milky, melting, orgasmic terror
And delight
Of Me.

I am forbidden
By my hidden joy
To heighten the intrigue
To trick myself through hide and seek
Out of the infinite burden
Of Me.

You!
O delicious, deceptive You
A joke to take the heat off
The awesome wonder
Of Me.

I hide in You
I take pleasure and pain
In You
For your pain cannot compare
With the dread of being
Only Me.

You who bring the shadow
Of forgetfulness
Somnambulistic You
To lull me into sweet enchantment
That I may not remember
Me
And the starkness of aloneness:
The terror of
Infinite Me.

Who Will Suckle Thee?

O Luminous Child
Born amid the conflict
In my soul
Who will suckle Thee?

They move around you
Lost in the enchantment
Of their own emotions.

Reaching
         Pulling
  Taking
          Breaking

Forsaking You
they do not see
An echo
Of their own desires.

Isn't it strange
What people do
With the image
Of your life?·

Here, come here.
O Thee,
I draw you gently
To my breast
And encircle you
In my embrace.

How good it feels
To hold you to my chest.
I am able
I am willing
I will suckle you
Until you are full.

Rest.
Rest in stillness
Until entheos
Breathes you into form.

Love's Changing Face

Love's changing face
If I may call it love
Leaves me aghast.
I tremble in confused terror
As I awaken from enchantment's dream
And wonder where I am
Or where I've been.

How can it be, this strangeness?
How can it be that I who have loved
Am now loveless and filled with a fury
Wrought by betrayal's underhand?
What is the alchemical magic
Whereby sweetness is changed into bitter pain
And softness into granite?

What Song Is This

What song is this that fills me with its loveliness
Until I am overfull
And intoxicated with my own fullness?
                       A bubble bursts
                       Water breaks
                       A child is born.
Through fleshy veils
A delirium of pain and blood
Slowly awakens me
To the reality of my own birth:
                       I give birth to myself!
How can it be?
How can it be that I a devotee of both,
Of you and me
Of Us
Can give birth within the realm of Myself
To a child that is an emerging dream
That embraces and encompasses
Vast regions of Rainbow Splendor?

O splendid Androgynous Dream!
The gift of relationship held within my hands
As I glimpse the meaning of the Golden Ball
And the beauty of Swan Walk.
                       Hold the ball and dance
                       smoothly in balanced Beauty.
The eyes within my hands perceive
They glide along the silken surface
The ball: the dream
     My eyed hands observing fragments of the total
        Emerging in the Magic Dance.

Kitchen Creek August 30

The seed desires to love myself
In every cranny and nook
I am the center of a kingdom vast
Author, pages and print of a grand book.
I am the texture of pages
The color of the print
Wafting through the ages
I am the delicate scent
Arising lightly as the volume opens
Fragrances of aging well
Vintage wine, nectar pure
Of whose wonder time will stories tell.

I am the Light
I am the Love
The vessel that embraces all
Uniquely intimate in every part
And aspect, great and small.

I am the wily, dragon wind
The cloud, a condensation.
I am the stillness of the night
I am visionary revelation

I am the Light
I am the Love
Embracing from within
I am the song of the Beloved's glance
I am the ensouled twin

I am the Dance
I am the Play
The movement of sheer delight
I am the prized unlimited thought
The divine soul-ship in flight.

God I am
God I am
God I am

Section V

The Circle Turns

Mystery

Let the light shine, Beloved,
A quiet flame that softly illuminates
The darkness with golden warmth;
A futile radiance whose moment
Of realization comes in the depth of midnight
And in the Mystery of the
Dark Moon.

The Circle Turns

The circle turns and once again
I find an empty boredom
It's over and there is nothing more to be said
Except, perhaps, good-bye.
Here we sit in utter fear, hyping beyond hype
That things are not what they seem
And yet it is clear There is nothing here
But empty fantasies gazing across a chasm
And lingering in atrophied dreams that never quite were
And never will be
For the worlds of you and me can never cross.
Thus the loss
The pain and bewilderment
Or simply the bewilderment of an unanswerable "Why?"

And sitting and sighing like an oracle of old
Objective and unmoved
I peer into the veil of future selves
And wonder what costumes there are now to be worn.
Shorn of my illusions I nakedly stand
And know that all the while
The feelings have never been wrong.
The fantasy of unity dissolves in the mists
And I wait silently for possible doorways
Into other unknown adventures.

March 29, 1986, Easter Eve

Of Magic

Mysterious songs
Borne on runic breath
Of Magic spell
Incantations
Living songs
Of flesh and blood
Emotive rainbow sounds
Of dancing flesh
Celebrating
The wonder
Of the Sacred Fire.

I Am

I sing to you of balance
But do you hear my song
Or merely the echoes
Of past memories:
Conclusions drawn and set
In final form for all time.

You speak of balance
As some kind of stasis
A static dead something.
How blind you seem to be.
The physical body in its
Awesome balance
An infinity of Yin-Yang in one:
Systole-diastole in-breathing out-breathing
Alkaline-acid
All dynamic movements of balance
All contained within One.

Even Kabir perceived:
I am a woman and the wife of God.

When I am in a place like this
Suspended, reserved, alone
A skillfully constructed instrument
Seemingly without a tone,
I wonder, knowing that it is all just fine,
Yet knowing this, wander down a line
Into a vast, suspended place
Without a face
Or subtle trace
Of who I was or am

But still I know
That I am
Within and outside of this moment of sensation
And now to seed a re-creation
That leads again to unknown places
Fashioning new and different faces
Truly reflecting an undiscovered me
Realized and free.

Future

The future opens before me.
A hesitant sun peeps over
The receding horizon
Splaying its pink and golden light
Upon the yawning landscape
Awakening to the possibilities
Of a new Day.

I see you in your sighing Beauty
And touch the quiet flame
Rising like a pillar of fire
From the center of your being
And illuminating the darkness
Of our veiled and frustrated yearning.

A river flows
A pregnant desert flowers
And gives birth to strange, delicious fruits.

Veils

Through veils of flesh
I touch the quiet fire
That burns within the center
Of your soul
And evokes memories
Of distant times
Wherein we slept and dreamed
The dream of Us,
Of you and me,
And in between:
Veiled worlds that are the body
Of our love.

Scorpio Moon

So like the face I thought you'd wear
Had you ever been you.
So like the way I thought you'd be
Had you ever been you.

So like the heart
I felt you'd be
Had you
ever been you.

But in you I find the far flung fragrance
Of a mysterious flower borne in the heart of me,
And though I smell and enjoy your scent
To touch you is an impossibility.

I imagine your body in the shape of you,
Scorpio moon and all.
I imagine your playful, mercurial strain
Your expanding rise and fall...

Perhaps again it seems like you
A you I want to be.
To attain the face that seems like you
But perhaps is only me.

Tightrope walking without a rope
Extended into space,
hoping without hope
With my own imagination.

A princely, noble face
That answers my soul's desire
My heartstrings' quivering melodies
Imprisoned in unknowing.

Free to drift upon the land
Like fingers gliding on skin
Knowing when
And how to be

Again with you
alive and free
As the ever turning
circle turns.

Friday

To open the brain is my heart's desire
A bold adventure to which I aspire
To live each moment in full joy—That I would
To live a completely open creature-hood.
A fully functioning receiver would have I
And ride the great wind with a gentle sigh.
A chameleon, with love, is what I would be
Shape-shifting, wholly alive and free.
Free from limitations of time and space
Free to roam exuberant from place to place
In richly woven style like a fine work of art
To know I'm myself and yet a great part
Of a vast splendid Kingdom, of Heaven, it's called
I wish to explore it, multi-dimensions, all.

And so from the Lord God of my Being I feel
I desire that this dream shall now become real.
From the soul of my being the quicksilver is stirred
Because the opening of the flower is preferred.
So shall it be written, so shall it be done
An adventurous life lived in nothing but fun.
I fully embrace and love what is me
Which opens and frees me to love what is thee.
Open the doors! Open the gates!
Free the hormones! Release the Fates!
So it is written, so shall it be done
Alive and living in Harmony—what fun!
And so it is!

A healer of dreams is what I would be
A light unto the world, luminous and free.
Oh let the runners come, let the learning begin
Awaken! Awaken, the Spirit of Friend.
So it is written, so shall it be done
Alive in the Kingdom, laughing in fun!
And so it is.

Poets Sing

Beloved:
The poets sing songs
Of ancient dreams, familiar times
Soft the candle's glow.

I watch as you sleep
Holy Bliss...holding you.
Uma is so kind.

Flaming water bed
The frantic, frisbee player
Searching for my soul.

Your soul's morning warmth
The aura of liquid gold
Waking up with you

I collect my tears
In Sparkletts water bottles
Just in case of drought

Tenderness rises
Like the multi-hued dawning
Of the morning sun.

Tender lips express
"How did you come into my life?"
Trembling, gentle wind.

Cool, crisp pre-dawn air
Richness of the loving night
Fills me with its kiss.

Cool canyons walk pass
Alone I pursue the dawn
Two would ease the task.

Thank you for the tear
That almost was a rainbow
Eye. Believe in Love!

Thank you for the tear
That almost was a rainbow.
I believe in Love.

The fresh morning air
Kisses you and misses you
Wishing you were here.

Above the misty canyon
The Black Raven soars and speaks
Echoing our hearts.

Above the misty canyon
Echoing our unity
Raven sings his song.

Spirit Descends

Through an open window the spirit descends
a broad-winged falcon
touches the earth.
Quicksilver presence
dances like moondust
from dream through physical reality's
penetrating gaze and ever deepening embrace.
A luminous mirror
reflects upon your Creative Play
chasing the wind across the canvas of my soul
I find you hidden in unsuspecting roles.

So easily you shed your forms.
A serpent sloughing its skins,
you refuse to be confined in time
always a mystery sublime.
And in delight
the soul takes flight
for a moment hovers upon an enigma
then glides upon the wind and out of sight.
My soul takes flight
upon a pinnacle of ecstasy
realizes the taste of tears
salty and sweet
melting the heart of the unknown.

My Name

I have a man, a spirit-husband, who shares my world and helps me create the aspects and ambiances that fulfill his being and mine. I am very deeply feminine and need a strongly masculine man to balance me in Creativity and Love in the service of Beauty.

I feel most at home when I can feel the deep places in myself: It brings life forth in me and in others. I need to bring forth Man for in that way I see and experience myself most clearly, richly and deeply.

I realize I am in a male body, yet my deeper reality is feminine to an extraordinary degree and I seek and have a man to bring that fulfillment. "There is no medicine man without a medicine woman. It has always been so."

I have a man, a spirit-husband, who shares in the fulfillment and growth of those deep places within my being for that is his fulfillment as well as mine. Our children are the Alchemy unfolding between us, which is a radiant vortex of catalytic living energy that ignites the world with Love and Beauty.

My name is Dark Waters for I am deep, mysterious and magical. I am agua vitae, I give life to all who drink of me. I am rich and full and transparent: agua radiante.

Of Ecstatic Wonder

I am man.
I perform the antics of life.
I am the actor on the stage.
I am the structure of the arena.
I am the form that gives meaning to substance.
I am the flame
That holds you enthralled
In supernal wonder;
The drying flame
That burns and sears;
The circle of flame
That protects and comforts.
I am the dying flame
That leaves you standing
Amidst the smoldering embers
Of ecstatic wonder.

I am a strong sun pillar
Unyielding yet giving
Of infinite light
That penetrates the darkest regions
Of your Divine Mystery.

I am a fiery sun
That transforms your moistness
Into visionary vapors
Of dawning realms
Wakeful dreams
Of golden liquid Light.

I am a proud warrior
A gentle hunter and protector.
I am a raging storm...
yielding in my hardness
Yet unreachable in my detachment.
Find me.

Beautiful Friend

It is now summer and I have watched and experienced an autumn meeting blossom into a summer of richness. Quietly and almost imperceptibly you have become a part of my world: You, a radiant light that penetrates the veil of my aloofness and finds me sleeping in the cavern of my aloneness. In a strange stillness I have come to an awakening of your tender caring and loving caress.

You always say "thank you" on departing. Now I say thank you. Thank you for being you. Thank you for being there. Thank you for being with me in the spaces we have shared thus far. Thank you for the way you let me know you are present. Thank you for the possibility of feeling in a new way; for the possibility of experiencing life in a familiar and yet different way. As I discover pottery I discover something of myself and you; something new and different. So too with the men's group. The seed of the idea was planted the night of our meeting at the Jung weekend.

I Hunger

I hunger and I thirst,
For I know not what:
Hissing, serpentine movements
Within the caverns
Of my infinite soul.

My thoughts cannot encompass
Nor my mind comprehend
My unsurpassed yearning and longing
For the presence
Of the Beloved of my Soul.

From the deep and infinite expanses
Of my cellular life
From the core of my existence
From the center of my center
I call to that one
That completes my Being.

Companions of my heart
Creature brothers and sisters
Of earth, air, water
Greening comrades, mineral comrades
Brother and sister creatures all
Whom Mother Earth has brought forth
Lend your compassion to my deep longing
And help me awaken the heart of my Beloved
That he might awaken and remember
The embracing harbor of my love
And the tender comfort of my caress
That he might become aware
Of the gestures hidden within me
And shaped to the contours
Of only Him.

O my Friends,
Perhaps I speak to you in madness
Yet that madness is my salvation
For in his love is my reality
And in my heart is His.

Sacred Dance

How can I tell you, my Love?
   How can I make you see
How it is that we
   Are meant to be
Together
   You and I
Let us try
   Let us fly
Into the spacious arms
   Of our embrace
Created through the blending
   Of our hearts in Love.

O Magic Wind
   Breathe upon our souls
With misty threads
   Spun of finest silver
Weave our hearts as one
   That we may dance
In Sacred realms
   Infusing time and space
With awe and wonder
   Of the Holy Mystery
Within:
         Within the depth of the cave
            Within the hopes and yearnings
         Within the blood, the sweat, the tears,
            Within the flowing rivers
         Of humanity's deepest desires
            Within the diamond dewy perspiration
         Of Love's embrace
            Within the fires of conflict and passion
         Within the heart of a Rose

A fragrance arises
   and fills the space
Without:
         Without you there is no song
            Without you incessant longing
            For simple dreams and happy times
               Wherein we experience
            The birth of the Divine
               Between your heart and mine
Within the embrace
   Of Love.

Kitchen Creek: Solstice

The spark is gone
No longer the Sacred Flame
That lights the path
To wonder and magic.
I struggle for rainbows
And find only continuous
Grey June opaque skies
And the realization
Of your dream come true.

> If you block the flow
> You will create a world of half-life
> Opaque and grey
> And I don't wish
> To live in greyness.

Mid-afternoon a walk
Along dusty trails
Leading to that sacred spot
Where once we made our bed
Beneath the pine.

As I approach
Crickets and locusts
Sing their heralding songs
Announcing the emergence
Of a memory,
The earth,
My soul,
One fabric, one piece
And here I stand
Beneath this tree
I touch the ground.

How strange is memory...
Dry leaves shatter
Underfoot—
Is this a cradle
Or a grave?
The fragrance
Of Autumn's reflection
And Winter's melody
Fills the air.
Spring's new growth
Blankets the past
And in my soul
A wind moves
In echoing wonder:
Was this a cradle
Or a grave?

Shades of Grey

My whole life has been lived mostly under a mantle of grey; the brooding of a storm ready to happen or the relentless grey of a weather front that decides to settle down in one's neighborhood. The opaque greys of yearnings almost or never fulfilled. The leaden greys that weigh you down if not physically, then emotionally and spiritually.

This limited exploration of grey in a possible rainbow color spectrum conditions one to a very narrow perspective of life and the ultimate interpretation that it really isn't worth it. The joyous times seem as miniscule as a snowflake and almost as fleeting (unless you reside in a cold climate) and anyway who wants to hang out in the frigid regions clutching for warmth, dying for the sake of a little relief.

As I grow older I am coming to a realization, embryonic throughout the whole of my life, that I really don't believe very much in life. With all the ballyhoo, with all the hype, with all the lip-smacking around things like food and sexuality, it just really isn't that appealing. It isn't fair. And moments generally dedicated to fantasizing and creating that sense of sustained joy inevitably dissolve into the amorphous, brooding greys. Yet, some do hang on for dear life whatever the cost. As I mature, I realize I'm not one of those. For I find that what's sunshine one day is a hurricane the next—so why bother? And that's a serious question.

Are we only creatures of make-believe, hoping against all hope that feelings and emotions of "value" truly do exist and are "eternal"? That somehow we can create and sustain a world of unlimited Joy, Peace, Love, Wonder, Beauty? Beneath all the make-believe and ballyhoo, I don't think so. And perhaps it isn't fair, and perhaps I'm looking for perfection, and perhaps I want to create life other than what it is. After years of striving, desiring, wanting and wishing to know, to be aligned and attuned with some purposeful order or meaning, I only find myself on a recurring wheel of the same old round of happy, sad; hopeful, hopes dashed; in "love," in pain. I stop, basta, surrender, give up, finito. I don't expect it to be any better. I don't hope for any miracles (Ha!). I don't hope to endure the present moments, expecting a new spring to sprout around the corner. No more roller-coaster. Simply, a robot upon whose strings emotions play out without any value as the seasons and the weather come and go oblivious to anything but their own rhythm. And tears, like rain falling, aren't sad; they are simply water falling. So what?

But, before I expire (if there's such a thing) I want to perceive myself "as I am."

I desire to play in the vivid color spectrum of the rainbow, from violet to red. So be it!

Down the Labyrinth

Man-child, listen to my song.

Down the labyrinth of time and space
Have I traveled
In search of the familiar
An aroma, a glance, a touch
A simple gesture
That reminds me of home.
I have wandered over unfamiliar
Landscapes
And searched the many worlds
In the hope of finding
That which is mine
From the Beginning.

Can you hear my song
Can you feel the current
Moving in Moonlight's
Mystical magical murmurings
Of Love's eternal call?
Can you grasp the unspeakable
That was before the Fall?

I'm a weary wanderer
Sent out upon the Wind
The sounds of magic making
That cause the worlds to blend
I seek the magic potion
That fills the empty part
I seek the truly other
To complement my heart.

The words I cannot tell you
If words they truly be.
The signs I cannot show you
For mortal eyes can't see
The nature of the splendor
The beauty of Light
The power of Darkness
The mystery of Night.

Can you hear my story
Can you hear my song
Can you feel the current
Of Love's eternal call?
Can you grasp the unspeakable
That was before the Fall?

Listen to the rhythm
Feel the pulsing beat
Touch the fertile magic
Sense the rising heat
Taste the glowing nectar
Smell the ruby rose
Grasp the holy secret
That it does disclose.

Within

In the winter of my love
I turn within and rest.
Amidst the harvest
Of my longing,
In winter sleep
I dream the dream
Of future seasons
Springing from the well
Of the Mystery
Within.

The Heart's Desire

Embraced within the middle ground
The interface between square and round,
Exuberant dancers ecstatically aspire
To know and fulfill the heart's desire.
Deep within the almond shape
Dancer rises to undrape
And in that moment does escape
Into the place of the Sacred Fires
Whose flickering flames the heart inspires.
She rises, unfolds and elaborates the dance
Awakening dreams and the wonder of chance.
Both near and far a vision seen clear,
The heart's desire is drawing near.
To live within Nature's full-bodied embrace
A sovereign being by Nature graced
With strong attunement existing in harmony
With the four elementals, alive and free.
Knowing wisely both within/without
And living simply without a doubt.
By Sun and Earth and Air and Sea
This dream shall in three-dimensionality be:
A homestead nestled in Nature's breast
Empathic alignment within its caress.
To live as one who plays with the wind
My body, the Earth; my body, My Friend.
Embracing the dream of the Immortal Elf
Simply and truly loving myself.
So it is written, so shall it be done
A marvelous adventure, exciting and fun.
Elegant movement, artistic expression
The creation of Beauty my daily profession.
Beauty created with unlimited Love.

Section VI

God's Gift

This was James' only book,
done as a chapbook
in the winter/spring of 1992.

God's Gift

by
James Stewart

I hold you and I am held
This is the poetry
And the weaving of a magic spell
This is the dragon's song...

Radha-Krishna,
Help me call the one
to touch the place
of desire
beyond the reach of words.

Help me soothe the quiet ache
of incessant longing
for only God knows what.
Touch me intimately
with the love of knowing
that I may unfold
the quivering bud
yearning to blossom
within.

Radha-Krishna,
I evoke the peace of love united
That I may live
The love I am within without.

God's Gift

A rooster crowed at the dawning of my realization
Cocksure plumage blowing in the wind
Chest broadly expanded readying to sing its greatest song.
Rooster's scratch unzips the costume of my ego
And with laser precision strips away the seven veils
Cloaking and Concealing the Chamber of the King
Inside the Great Octahedron.
Rooster crows
Ego screams
Brilliant, ruffled plumage dances in the wind.
Rooster's crow
Ego's mantramic, "NO!"
Blend into celebratory sounds
Heralding the dawning of a new day
The seeding of a new way
Of being
Me

A Future Me

A future me embraces the wind
And breathes a song whose melody
Inseminates my past and present lives.
Unearthing a continuum of memory
That underlies and unifies
Past and present I's.
And which awakens me to the possibility
Of restructuring past and present me
Like a poem rewritten and given a different face
A different ordering in time and space
Nuances that inspire with the reality
Of the ultimate power of a future me
To create that which I may presently be
The way I thought the past could do
When I believed the power of the past was true.

But now I see it is a future me
Weaving a beautiful tapestry
And shaping my present into poetry
Spoken in some present/future now
As times and places gently allow
Whose garments bear the signature
Of a Taoist artist-sage
Who writes incisive poetic prose upon a textured page.
His subtle, exquisite artistry
The lilting fragrance of a human flower
Blossoming with exuberant joy in
Spring's recurring hour
Continually reminding me
To embrace life fully and be wholly free
Whose varied, shimmering summer hues
Kaleidoscopic blend of red, yellow and blues
Inspire the landscape with Muse-ical flight;
Whose fruit becomes rare, delicious wine
Bringing rapturous visions of sheer delight.

You Remind Me

You remind me of someone I used to know
In a never-ending "once upon a time"
Whose radiant presence instigates creative flow
Like the magical moonlit movement of a mime.

You remind me of someone I've felt before
In the ever-present days of never-when
And in the mystical embrace of evermore
It doesn't matter where we're going or where we've been.

You remind me of someone I've seen before
In the shadow of the Light that ever shines
Whose presence now calls us to blend and explore
Other avenues of pattern and designs.

You remind me of someone I used to sense
Approaching my tabernacle from afar
Carrying the seed of Primal evidence
Substantiating clearly who we are.

You remind me of someone I need to be
To feel the passion filling up the night
Whose steady presence calls me to be free
And let the future memories make it right.

You remind me of someone I use to feel
In dreams to be fulfilled within the now
You carry within you the matching seal
And touch which activates the fated vow.

You remind me of all I am and want to be
As I hold the future in the present now
The past is disengaged and I now am free
To become all things the present will allow.

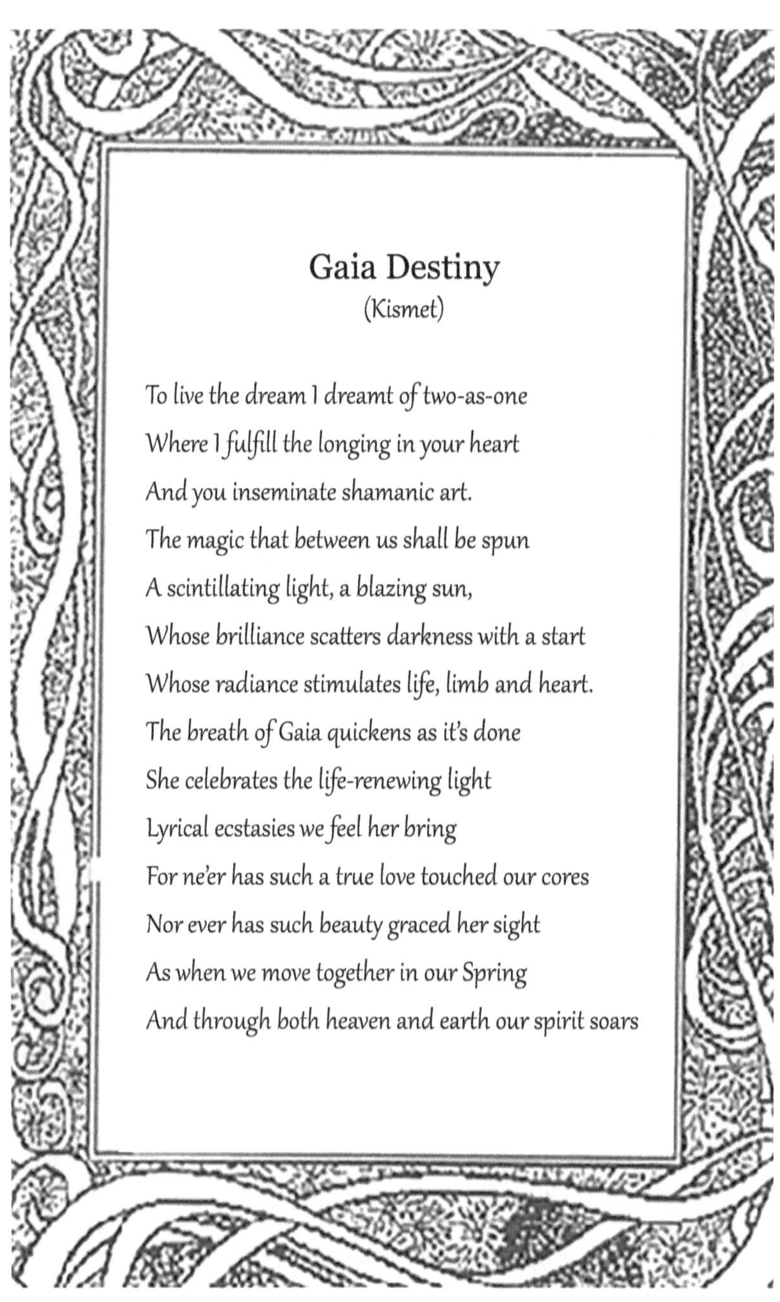

Gaia Destiny
(Kismet)

To live the dream I dreamt of two-as-one

Where I fulfill the longing in your heart

And you inseminate shamanic art.

The magic that between us shall be spun

A scintillating light, a blazing sun,

Whose brilliance scatters darkness with a start

Whose radiance stimulates life, limb and heart.

The breath of Gaia quickens as it's done

She celebrates the life-renewing light

Lyrical ecstasies we feel her bring

For ne'er has such a true love touched our cores

Nor ever has such beauty graced her sight

As when we move together in our Spring

And through both heaven and earth our spirit soars

God Has Given

A presence arises and descends
A shimmering emanation suffuses my world
With amber bronze radiance
Highlighting moments of golden joy
And remembrances of future times
Sequenced in sensuous wonder and pristine delight
In living in union and harmony
Within the Presence of Life
Before the worlds began.

A thousand years of longing
Congeal into a place called Home
As the times and half-times are fulfilled
And pass away.
Now, today, a capstone placed upon the pinnacle
Of the Great Pyramid ·
Signals the Return of the King.

I touch the threads of light
So beautifully woven into the sinew
Of your immaculate body
And breathe the subatomic intensity
Of Prana billowing between
The illusion of our separateness
And the sacred union of our singular soul.

Recognition

Time slips into the past
spontaneously the future
pours into our presence
a spring mountain stream
sparkling cool
refreshes the moment
with the radiance
of a future light
calling us to remember
the gift of two as one pristine
that penetrates the veils
which once upon a time
obscured the light
within

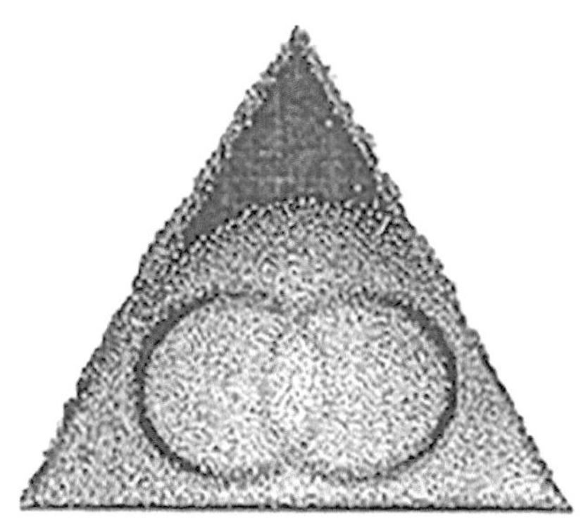

Trembling pines moan and sigh
silhouetted in the light of love this day
when by the winds caressed.
Tender lips riding breath
trace contours of fingertips into the soul
of one he loves the best.

Holding fast I trace the pristine line
the soft contour of your aesthetic spine.
My arms full round a galloping steed's nape
My body molds to every line and every shifting shape.
Holding fast I breathe with you
passionate in flight.
Holding fast I seed with you
dreams that reunite.

Things Not Said...

Things not said
Words unspoken
Protect a heart
Afraid of being broken.
Hesitantly I stand before you
calculating a camouflage
Lest passion possesses
And I find myself
Propelled and lost
In the fabric of your embrace
That special place
That echoes the song of my own heart
Grown overfull and rich
While we are seemingly apart.
I fall too easily
Like multiple waves
Breaking upon a shore
Intrigued I desire to explore
This unspeakable feeling
That eludes my concepts and words
Except perhaps for a banal "I love you"
An unsatisfying cliche.
And unsatisfied I yearn
To feel the presence, the weight , the texture
Of your steady essence which alters me
Even as I reach to touch
I am reinvented in the aura of your light

And on this tonight
I want to lie
Quietly near and simply sigh
Like a generic contented cow
As long as time and space allow
To linger in the here and now
Enfolding and unraveling the we
You and I alone and free
To feel, experience and be
What words cannot hold
A luminous essence of purest gold
A light transforming who we are
Again
Lest I shield and contort my need
Passion and desire must be freed
You are becoming indispensable
That in itself is not sensible.
Yet I know what I desire
And you are the closest to the Sacred Fire
present in my life.

Jewel in the Lotus

Dancing the dance of forever bliss
questors find their resting place.
Echoes of the serpent's hiss
resonate through timeless space.

Om mani padme hum.
all is sacred in the womb
Om mani padme hum.
all is forgiven in the tomb.

Sounds that sightless light become
drenching lovers in even sway
which to the serpent's sound succumb
heightening the roundelay.

Om mani padme hum.
smell the fragrant, sweet perfume
Om mani padme hum.
feel the budding flowers bloom.

Jewel in the Lotus, ah!
endless moment pervading time
sweet, exquisite baklava
savored with a hint of rhyme.

Om mani padme hum.
riding on a witches' broom
Om mani padme hum.
dancing within the womb-tomb.

Light's suffusing colors heat
rising passions cool the deep
heightening the rhythmic beat
frozen frameworks thaw and seep.

Om mani padme hum.
circling of the bride and groom
Om mani padme hum.
warp and woof upon a loom.

When the sweetness of the dance
presses towards the edge of bliss
relax control and take the chance
surrender to the serpent's kiss.

Om mani padme hum.
don't stay in the anteroom
Om mani padme hum.
and the tomb becomes the womb.

Jewel in the Lotus, stay
as it was it now shall be
Lotus around the Jewel, play
Both united, both are free.

Om mani padme hum.
and the dead we shall exhume
Om mani padme hum.
and the world we shall illume.
Om mani padme hum.
Om mani padme hum.
Om mani padme hum.
Om

Time (less) You

...Twilight and evening bell
and after that the dark...

I do rather well in the brilliance of day
but in the descending light of twi
a spell is cast upon timeless shores;
a magical sound creating desire
for a remembered future place called home
an arbor where future dreams congeal
into tender moments of forever feelings
imbuing the heart
with rainbow auras of enchantment.

You hold before me promised dreams
of two ecstatically living as one.
Confluent streams flowing peerless and pristine
interfacing never done.
In the echo of quiet whispers
sensate rivers of knowledge glide
through subterranean canyons deep
within my soul expectant feelings
delight in living consistently
in the radiance of your love.

Moments drenched with eternity's dream
never quench my quenchless thirst
And though fulfilled for an instance, it seems
good-byes bring uncontrollable longing first.
A heart filled with mementos of togethering
insatiably yearns for what your presence brings.
And though inside I know
there is no thing called separation

still my world somehow contracts and I drown in obfuscation
as you disappear into another place within this time
absence from your presence somehow feels like such a crime.
Yet in all the love you've given, it's your presence that I lack.

Before the farewells are dispersed it seems I want you back
— the sound of you, the feel of you
the touch of you somehow
the breath of you
the smell of you
the quiet of you right now.
And lately, it's the shape of you
the vision you've become
in the inward sight that feels for you
the visioner has succumbed.
And holding you in quiet embrace
discovers a forever place
and how much more there is
to feel in love...

Gratitude

I am bathed in the sweat of the Power of Love
In tender moments of quiet ecstasy.
Candle flames undulate
Soft rhythms of moonlit meadows
Breathing in luminous silver light.
Winds arise and whisper
Melodies through golden reeds
And rustling trees pine away
Another dying of a day.
The birth of kisses
The taste of the vine.

Divine quivering lips drink the honey song
Of sweet delight.
Birds take flight
Singing blues
And golden bronze sunsets
Merge in purple hues
That light our loins
In heartfelt magic dance.

Your fragrance rises
Like the sweetness of blossoming flowers
And as we while away the hours
Intoxicates my soul with memories
Spun from spider's silk
That weaves our souls as one.

For who you are
For what you are
And that I am
My heart rejoices and overflows
Melting crystal tears clear serpentine passages
Leading toward the door
Where He stands in splendor within our hearts
And seals the promise of our knowing.

For You Who Live in the Mirror

I'm glad today we walked
I'm happy that we talked
somehow something has changed
the sub-atomic rearranged.
I stumbled through muddled speech
neophyte musician, the scratch and screech
not saying all I wished to say
"why did I get up today?"
Like an uncaged bird
my heart resonates
the sound of feeling heard.

My bungling speech the primitive sounds
of intimate, heartfelt desires
needing to be expressed for you
for me as my soul requires.
Like a sculptor struggling to shape a stone
or a singer meditating to find the right tone
or a poet blending word, rhythm and rhyme
to give birth to multifaceted beauty in time...
Yet I feel refreshed, my intention received
my life force welcomed, my silence believed
held gently by your sensuous grace
the life in me finds a receptive place.

You are important to me
You are important for me.
Yet I don't understand this fire.
I feel no purpose except the desire
of the life in me
to know itself in the presence of thee
and to realize—to real-ize
that thing so hidden
as to only be seen in your eyes.

It was important for me to be
this day with you.
It was important for me to see
this day with you
the blossoming life between
You and I retrieving the Unseen.

Nostalgia

We tuck away our memories
Like stories to be told when we are old
About the life we once knew
But which now seems to elude us
And exclude us
From its magical flight
As we go on into the night.

Is this what we are meant to be
Museums of sun-bleached memories
That remind us of what has been
As we pass our nows in half-lit corridors
Walking in the shadows of future possibilities
Lost in the fragrances
Of unforgettable yesterdays
Fading, once fashionable, but not totally forgotten
Tucked away in a closet,
Behind a door,
In a haunted house,
On a street
Whose name we can hardly
Remember?

Home

Home is your hand upon my heart
and your presence within my soul.
Home is your breath upon my fingertips
Billowing through the fabric of my being.
Home is being held in your encompassing embrace
Home is holding you within and without.
Home is the gentleness of your receptivity and
the innocence of your permeability.
Home is your gentle fingers secretly drawing me toward you.
Home is touching you and melting into the web-work
Of your sensuous body.
Home is feeling sacred threads of light weaving us as one.
Home is the way you give me space to fall in love with you.
Home is your steady strength that melts my heart and calls me
into remembrance of the symbol that we are
complete and whole.
Home is expressing I love you in a thousand ways for the
thousand years we were apart.
Home is being home with you until we are fulfilled.
Home is feeling united even when we are physically apart.
Home is touching you,
holding you,
breathing you,
drinking you,
speaking you,
feeling you,
seeing you.
Home is being you and me, I and thee,
as it was in the beginning
It is now and ever...
World of you and me without end. Om;m;m;m;m;m;m.

Still Life

To imagine that you are here
Steady, close—"O God, so near!"
These are feelings to be arrayed
Through the Eye in the soul, not delayed
But played upon
We realize that we are one.

Let's be still
Then walk and talk
As we wander down pathways of forever
Generated by quiet sighs
Breathing upon intimate landscapes
Vividly shimmering into sensate view
Texture and hue
Of emotional nuance
Weaving future tales long forgotten
Now well remembered
In the billowing warmth of you and I
Reweaving the tattered tapestry
From when we fell apart.

Let's be still
And allow the magnetic threads
To discover connecting places
Let's give birth to familiar faces
Borne upon nostalgia's future
Woven on the loom
Of an ever-present Love
That births our seamless dream.
No longer you and I
We live as one, not two
We are what we say
We weave what we do.

Alhambra

Through the palace of the heart
crimson fingers reach into the dreamtime
to touch the miracle of you and I
within and without
held each inside the other's embrace.

Before the heart of truth I stand revealed
My cloaks removed
yes, I admit that you and I...
are one.

Things Not Said...

It is not the past we feel
As the veils of our heart unfold
But future memories touching our soul
With a passion to be born "once upon a time."

I touch the possibility
Of a radiance we have never known
And weep in joy for the manifesting dream come true.
I love you from a future place and time
That words cannot reach nor thoughts fabricate
A place realized only in the ecstasy
Of our heart rejoicing in Magic Dance,
The living chance.

Just Like This

I wanted to be embraced, Just like this
Your arms so full and firm around me, Just like this
Convey the need to hold/be held, Just like this
Intense, magnetic, illuminating passion, Just like this.

Is the holding held too long Just like this?
Oh no, my mind, hold on! Hold on! Just like this
Floating in a shimmering sea—an ecstasy—Just like this
Relaxing pleasure drifts in diamond light. Just like this.

Subtle warmth feels supple sinew, Just like this
Heads curl down on waiting shoulders, Just like this
Be still and let the sounds emerge, Just like this
Melt the heart of winter snow, Just like this.

"Is this too long to hold, be held? Let go! Hold on! Just like this
Don't drink too much. Don't glut the sea
Remember 'decorum'—how one is to be."
"Oh no, no, no, my simple mind, this is my time to see...and be"
Just like this.
Just like this
Rediscovering my pores as gills and loving to breathe
The breath of you
The breath of me
The seamless breathing of I and Thee
Just like this
Just like this
Just like this.

"I saw a hawk
and thought of you..."

Uprising silence within the One
two unfold their wings for flight
darkness dissolves in luminous light
a new song has begun.

I desire to explore the dream state. I want to be able to be clearly and precisely oriented in the dreamscape without the conscious attitudes/beliefs distorting my perceptions when I return from dream travel. At present I feel the waking state too heavily restrictive, narrow and one dimensional. When I awake I can feel the dream disappearing, I believe, because of attitudes, beliefs and constrictions of my conscious waking stance.

This may be as it should be and needed for appropriate orientation to my current time and place of being in three dimensional reality. Yet I feel with practice and modification this condition can be improved upon and be re-created with more flexibility, give and take, and multifacetedness. I want to change this current state and to molt the waking framework's foundation so as to facilitate memory, clear perception and description of dream experience.

For example, I wish to increase the multifaceted ability of my waking consciousness so that more than one channel of material can be handled without distortion or undue constriction. Perhaps to imagine a room/garden/place where things are more open-ended; or perhaps I could imagine siting at a control panel which would give me initially, controlled access to dreamscape experiences with accuracy and precision of communication. And gradually as I make the necessary changes in my perceptions, my images and experiences would be less mechanically oriented.

I desire to be awake and conscious in the dream world and retain a strong sense of identity, yet with the flexibility to shift shape and orient to a multileveled landscape and perceive clearly along many channels simultaneously. For example, like singing and playing the piano at the same time.

I desire to develop inner senses. I desire that the ego, the waking ego, co-operate in this venture somewhat as has happened on psychedelic experiences. I want the ego to become so familiar with the potential of these developments and states that I feel "at home" and not threatened.

When you explore the inside of a concept, you act it out.

My Name

I have a man, a spirit-husband, who shares my world and helps me create the aspects and ambiances that fulfill his being and mine. I am very deeply feminine and need a strongly masculine man to balance me in Creativity and Love in the service of Beauty.

I feel most at home when I can feel the deep places in myself: it brings life forth in me and in others. I need to bring forth Man for in that way I see and experience myself most clearly, richly and deeply.

I realize I am in a male body, yet my deeper reality is feminine to an extraordinary degree and I seek and have a man to bring that fulfillment. "There is no medicine man without a medicine woman. It has always been so."

I have a man, a spirit-husband, who shares in the fulfillment and growth of those deep places within my being for that is his fulfillment as well as mine. Our children are the Alchemy unfolding between us, which is a radiant vortex of catalytic living energy that ignites the world with Love and Beauty.

My name is Dark Waters for I am deep, mysterious and magical. I am agua vitae, I give life to all who drink of me. I am rich and full and transparent: agua radiante.

James Stewart

www.ingramcontent.com/pod-product-compliance
Lightning Source LLC
Chambersburg PA
CBHW021204130726
47988CB00002B/504